The outdoor table

GREAT NEW ZEALAND EATING FOR GARDEN, BALCONY + BEACH

written and photographed by Garth Hokianga

PENGUIN
BOOKS

ACKNOWLEDGEMENTS

To the team at Penquin Books for their confidence,
persistence and support: Bernice Beachman who pointed
me in the right direction and Philippa Gerrard who guided
me along the way; brilliant word and ideas people.

Athena Sommerfeld, the designer of the book, who made
everything look so good. Athena thanks for putting up
with a control freak.

Special thanks to the ingredients people for their advice:
Dave at Top Cuts Butchery, Barry at The Fruit Shed,
Bruce Young at Moana Pacific Seafoods and Joe
Jakievich at Glengarry Wines.

Thanks most of all to Belinda, who endured the house
being filled to the brim with plates, food, camera gear
and really loud music.

The outdoor table

GREAT NEW ZEALAND EATING FOR GARDEN, BALCONY BEACH

garth hokianga

PENGUIN
BOOKS

I'll be honest with you. I first started cooking to get
out of fishing. My father was a crayfisherman and the
3 a.m. starts, coupled with childhood seasickness, sent
me searching for some other way to help. Cooking the
oversize crayfish, too big to sell at the markets, became
my way of pitching in, and to this day, fresh leg meat in
white bread still takes some beating in my opinion.
Sharing the bounty with the neighbourhood gave me my
first inkling into just how much everyone loves to be
cooked for and, even after fifteen years as a professional
chef, that's still what gets me going.

I've cooked almost everywhere. From a Hungarian bakery
run by a former Olympic wrestler, to an army tent pitched
at a police crime scene. From five-star restaurants and
royal kitchens, to a paddock without power or running
water. Fortunately, I'd outgrown the seasickness by the
time I began working back-to-back summers on the super
yachts that follow the sun. I once went six years without
a single winter and that endless summer feeling is what
I've tried to bring to this book. I can't control the
weather, but I can cook up the kind of dishes that send
your taste-buds to the beach even if it's bucketing down.

Summer is a splendid time to be cooking, but there
are days in every season that draw you outside. This
cookbook is designed to get you out of the kitchen and
into the great outdoors, with movable feasts perfectly
complimented by a roaring surf, a babbling brook, a
scenic mountain top, a lush meadow or a rustic picnic
table.

Outdoor fare, to me, combines intensity with simplicity.
These recipes are easy to prepare and even easier
to eat. This isn't fussy food – it is hands-on, simple
cooking, where the taste does all the talking. Many

of the recipes take only minutes to prepare, and quite a few of the desserts can be whipped up the day before, allowing the flavours to get on a first-name basis with each other in the fridge overnight.

Flavour is 'King' and generally one twist per dish is enough. After years of creating handstands on a plate, I have come back to the basics. In this book I have concentrated on real old-fashioned flavours and harked back to the classic combinations that Mother Nature designed to go together.

I have incorporated the very best from my travels and tastings, and at least twenty countries are represented in the recipes that fill the following pages. If I can give you any advice in the cooking of these dishes, it is to relax. By making the cooking process as relaxing as the eating, your food will turn out better. Honestly, preparing a meal is seldom a life or death situation and enjoyment adds a delicate yet delicious flavour, while stress is merely bitter.

If you're going to fuss over anything, it should be the raw ingredients you choose. A good chef demands the best and recognises it when they get it. Use all your senses when you're shopping: squeeze, sniff and eyeball until you're satisfied.

You will notice I've also harked back to some New Zealand classics that deserve to be remembered. While pikelets, pavlova and mint sauce can all be store-bought, nothing beats the real deal. As an edible connection with the past, these pure Kiwi tastes bring childhood memories alive with every bite.

CLASSIC COMBINATIONS

* tomatoes & basil
* plums & ginger
* mushrooms & bacon
* avocados & garlic
* blue cheese & raspberries
* bananas & rum
* smoked salmon & eggs
* prawns & pineapple
* scallops & bacon
* potatoes & Gruyère
* anchovies & cos lettuce
* tuna & artichokes
* asparagus & eggs
* venison & rocket
* beef & sour cream
* lamb & pinenuts
* chicken & cumin
* rhubarb & strawberries
* walnuts & sugar
* strawberries & vanilla
* chocolate & whisky
* saffron & rice
* white wine & shellfish

sangria cha cha

Life doesn't get any better than this: lounging on the grass, stuffing your face with food. But before you head outdoors, keep these tips in mind:

* When packing food to take outdoors, place the items in the chilly bin in the opposite order to which you will be serving them, i.e, the food you need last should be packed at the bottom. Take out the food only as you need it. Repack the chilly bin carefully and keep it in a shady spot.

* Pack food straight from the refrigerator to the chilly bin just before leaving home. Stow it in the coolest part of the car.

* You can make your own ice packs by filling clean, empty, plastic milk containers with water and freezing. Containers of ice last longer than bags of ice cubes.

* To keep hot foods such as soup or stew at their hottest for longer, fill your Thermos with boiling water and let it stand for a few minutes to heat up. Empty before filling with the hot food.

* Always be extra careful with foods that can spoil easily in the heat of the sun, especially shellfish and dishes with mayonnaise in them.

* Make sure frozen desserts such as ice-creams and sorbets are well frozen and packed into the bottom of the chilly bin wrapped in newspaper.

* Fish, poultry and meat should be thoroughly thawed before cooking, then well cooked. The centre of hamburger patties should not be pink, and the juices of all cooked foods should run clear. Use a clean plate when removing the cooked food from the grill.

* To prevent meat from charring on the barbecue, trim visible fat from cuts like lamb chops as this is what causes the flare-ups.

* It is always a good idea to make an 'exploratory' cut into any patties, poultry, meat or fish to check 'doneness'.

* All leftovers should immediately go back into the cooler where there is plenty of ice. If in doubt, throw it out.

* For foods designed to be served cold such as chicken salads, make sure you prepare them with cold ingredients. For example, the cooked poultry should be allowed to cool before it is added to the rest of the salad ingredients.

PICNIC CHECKLIST

* blanket or tablecloth
* umbrella & cushions
* napkins, paper or cloth
* paper towels for the cleanup
* forks, knives & spoons
* serving utensils
* cake slice
* plates & bowls
* wine & water glasses
* corkscrew & bottle opener
* tea towels
* ice packs
* can opener
* small cutting board & knife
* portable sauce favourites
* savoury crackers
* cookies
* salt & pepper
* sugar & milk
* water, juices & alcohol
* thermos for hot liquids
* portable radio
* 1 chilly bin for beverages & 1 for perishable food
* rubbish bags
* sunscreen & hats
* insect repellent or citronella candles
* matches or lighter

shopping list

FRESH FOOD

* red onions
* limes
* mangoes
* strawberries
* raspberries
* blueberries
* avocados
* cos lettuce
* rocket lettuce
* peppers
* asparagus
* apricots
* pineapple
* plums
* peaches
* limes
* nectarines
* fresh corn
* vine-ripened tomatoes
* Parmesan
* fresh mozzarella
* buttermilk
* sour cream
* yoghurt
* lime leaves
* fresh ginger
* basil
* coriander
* oregano
* thyme
* mint
* parsley
* lemongrass
* garlic
* lemons
* cherry tomatoes
* ham piece
* eggs
* fresh fish

PANTRY FOOD

* rum
* tequila
* canned beetroot
* canned tomatoes
* canned beans
* tofu
* Maldon sea salt
* gherkins
* roasted red peppers
* pickled artichokes
* pickled onions
* capers
* olives
* basmati rice
* Kikkoman soy sauce
* rice vinegar
* horseradish sauce
* Dijon mustard
* maple syrup
* tomato paste
* tomato sauce
* tobasco sauce
* sherry vinegar
* Kewpie mayonnaise
* honey
* sumac
* ground white pepper
* cumin
* cardamom
* cinnamon
* olive oil
* grape seed oil
* peanut oil
* pinenuts
* walnuts
* cocoa powder
* chocolate
* almonds

FREEZER FOOD

* prawns
* boneless chicken breasts
* chicken wings
* ground beef mince
* beef fillets
* bacon
* sausages
* lamb racks
* baguettes
* puff pastry
* plain sponge cake
* vanilla ice-cream
* frozen blueberries

THIS BOOK IS FOR BELINDA

contents

one | home-made sauces

TOMATO SAUCE

Prep 90 minutes
Makes 3 cups

1 tablespoon olive oil
1 large onion, peeled and chopped
2 cloves garlic, peeled and finely chopped
2 cans whole peeled tomatoes with juice
½ cup tomato paste
1 tablespoon sugar
1 cup red wine
1 bay leaf
2 tablespoons fresh basil, chopped
1 tablespoon fresh oregano, chopped
½ teaspoon salt
freshly ground black pepper to taste

In a saucepan over medium heat add the oil, onion and garlic and sauté until soft.

Add all the remaining ingredients, breaking up the large pieces of tomato with a wooden spoon.

Bring the sauce to the boil, reduce heat and simmer. Cook for 60 minutes, uncovered, until the sauce reduces to 3 cups.

Remove the bay leaf and cool sauce at room temperature. Cover and store in the refrigerator. Will keep for 5 days, or freeze for up to 3 months.

Every summer my Mum would spend days in the kitchen making huge batches of tomato sauce. I don't really have the room to store dozens of jars of 'tom' sauce, so I prefer to make a small batch as I need it and keep it in the fridge as one of my summer sauce standbys.

BBQ SAUCE

Prep 40 minutes
Makes 5 cups

2 tablespoons butter
1 large red onion, peeled and chopped
3 cloves garlic, peeled and chopped
2 cups canned tomatoes with juice
2 cups water
½ cup tomato sauce
4 tablespoons red wine vinegar
3 tablespoons Worcestershire sauce
2 tablespoons honey
2 tablespoons Dijon mustard
3 teaspoons chilli powder
salt and freshly ground black pepper to taste

In a saucepan over medium heat melt the butter, add the onion and garlic and cook for 4 minutes until soft.

Add the tomatoes and water and simmer for 10 minutes, then add the remaining ingredients and simmer for another 20 minutes, stirring occasionally.

Transfer the mixture to a food processor and purée until silky smooth, then season to taste.

Pour into a bowl and allow the sauce to cool before storing, covered, in the refrigerator.

Great as a basting sauce or as your summer table sauce. This sauce is also a good base for other flavours such as minced ginger, lemon zest or liquid smoke.

bbq sauce

SESAME AND PARSLEY SAUCE

Prep 10 minutes
Makes 1½ cups

¾ cup tahini paste (ground sesame seeds)
½ cup lemon juice
1 clove garlic, peeled and minced
3 tablespoons water
1 cup Italian parsley, roughly chopped
salt and freshly ground black pepper to taste

Place the tahini paste, lemon juice and garlic into a food processor and purée until smooth.

If the mixture is too thick, add a few tablespoons of water, one at a time, and process until it thins to the desired consistency.

Add the parsley and salt and pepper to taste and pulse until blended. Store, covered, in the refrigerator.

Great served with salads, baked fish or as a sauce base for pizza. Italian parsley has a stronger and more peppery flavour than curly parsley.

FRESH PLUM SAUCE

Prep 90 minutes
Makes 1½ cups

2 cups plums, pitted and quartered
1 cup white sugar
1 cinnamon quill
1 heaped tablespoon fresh ginger root,
  peeled and chopped
2 tablespoons white rice vinegar
pinch salt
cold water

For this sauce, make sure you use a stainless-steel pan, not cast iron, as the vinegar will react and make your plum sauce taste like metal. In a medium-sized saucepan over a low heat add the plums, sugar, cinnamon, ginger, vinegar and a pinch of salt and cook until thick and syrupy – this will take about 1 hour.

Cool at room temperature for 30 minutes, then remove the cinnamon quill.

Purée in a food processor until smooth. At this stage you can add cold water to adjust sauce thickness. You would thin this sauce down more if you were going to use it as a dipping sauce, for example. Store, covered, in the refrigerator.

This sauce is very tasty with any grilled meats, but is at its best with Christmas ham or barbecued prawns. I'm a big fan of white rice vinegar, as it has a gentler sharpness than cider – give it a go.

NECTARINE BUTTER

Prep 30 minutes
Makes 1½ cups

4 large egg yolks
⅔ cup white sugar
1 cup nectarines, stoned and puréed
  in a food processor
juice of 1 lemon
½ teaspoon rose water
3 tablespoons butter, diced small

In a stainless-steel bowl whisk the egg yolks with the sugar, nectarine purée, lemon juice and rose water.

Place bowl over simmering water and whisk ingredients constantly until thickened. Be careful not to overcook at this stage or you will scramble the egg yolks.

Remove from heat and beat in the butter, a little at a time. You can strain the fruit butter if you wish, but I don't as I like the added taste of the nectarine skins. Store in a covered bowl in the refrigerator and serve chilled.

Make sure your nectarines are very ripe, or experiment and try other stone fruits such as peaches. Use this fruit butter on muffins, in chicken salads or in sweet pastry tarts for picnics.

fresh plum sauce

grilled pepper salsa

CHUNKY RHUBARB SAUCE

Prep 30 minutes
Makes 1 cup

1 tablespoon oil
1 medium-sized onion, peeled and diced
5 rhubarb stalks, trimmed, peeled and cut into chunks
1 tablespoon fresh ginger, peeled and finely chopped
3 cloves garlic, peeled and thinly sliced
1 bay leaf
3 tablespoons sugar
3 tablespoons cider vinegar
salt and freshly ground black pepper to taste

In a saucepan over low heat add the oil and cook the onion for 10 minutes until soft, stirring occasionally. Add the rhubarb, ginger, garlic and bay leaf. Stir gently with a wooden spoon for 10 minutes, until rhubarb is soft but not broken up.

Add the sugar and vinegar and cook for about 7 more minutes until the rhubarb is completely cooked but still chunky. Season with salt and freshly ground black pepper.

Remove the bay leaf, give the sauce one more taste test for sweetness and tartness and adjust to your own personal taste. You can serve this sauce either warm or cold.

I like to serve this sauce with savoury meat dishes like roast duck, chicken, venison or wild pork. If you are serving it warmed, add a little marsala, sherry or cognac to round out the flavours and give it a bit of zip.

GRILLED PEPPER SALSA

Prep 20 minutes
Makes 2 cups

2 large red peppers, roasted and diced
2 large yellow peppers, roasted and diced
1 tablespoon olive oil
1 tablespoon tobasco sauce
2 large tomatoes, diced

1 small red onion, finely chopped
2 cloves garlic, peeled and minced
2 tablespoons honey
juice of 2 limes
2 tablespoons coriander, finely chopped
½ teaspoon salt

Turn the oven onto a grill setting. To grill your peppers, cut in half and discard the core and seeds.

Lay pepper sides flat on an oven tray. Paint both sides with oil and grill for 5 minutes each side. At this stage peeling the peppers is optional. I don't bother as long as I don't burn the skins. Dice roughly.

Put all the ingredients into a bowl and mix with a wooden spoon. Store for up to 5 days, covered, in the refrigerator.

Peppers grown outdoors definitely taste sweeter than glasshouse peppers and they have twice as much Vitamin C.

real mint sauce

mushroom sauce

REAL MINT SAUCE

Prep 10 minutes
Makes 1 cup

2 cups mint leaves
½ cup cider vinegar
½ cup water
4 tablespoons white sugar
salt and white pepper to taste

Place the mint leaves (no stalks) into a food processor and pulse for 2 minutes until finely chopped. Scrape the sides down if necessary.

In a saucepan over medium heat add the cider vinegar, water and sugar. Stir with a wooden spoon until the sugar is dissolved, then bring to the boil.

Pour the hot liquid into the food processor with the mint and process for 30 seconds. Transfer to a bowl and season with salt and pepper. Serve at room temperature. Store, covered, in the refrigerator.

I love to serve this sauce with roast lamb and new season's potatoes or try it with battered seafood. For something a little different, add a cup of freshly peeled pineapple when processing the mint.

LEMON AND LIME SAUCE

Prep 10 minutes
Makes 1 cup

¼ cup lemon juice
juice and zest of 1 lime
¼ cup white sugar
½ cup water
1 tablespoon chilli powder
2 garlic cloves, peeled and finely chopped
3 fresh kaffir lime leaves

Put all the ingredients into a small saucepan and stir with a wooden spoon until the sugar is dissolved.

Place the saucepan on a medium heat and bring to the boil. Remove from heat and cool to room temperature.

Chill the sauce for at least 2 hours in the refrigerator before using.

This sauce gets better as it ages. Twenty-four hours will allow the oils in the lime leaves to infuse into the sauce. I use it as a quick dressing or dipping sauce for crispy foods such as spring rolls. It will keep for 2 months in the refrigerator.

MUSHROOM SAUCE

Prep 20 minutes
Makes 2 cups

1 tablespoon olive oil
1 medium-sized onion, peeled and chopped
2 garlic cloves, peeled and finely chopped
4 cups chopped mushrooms, any type
1 cup white wine
½ cup lemon juice
2 tablespoons sour cream (low fat)
salt and freshly ground black pepper to taste

In a saucepan over medium heat add the oil, onion, garlic and mushrooms and sauté for 5 minutes until golden brown.

Deglaze the pan with white wine, then add the lemon juice. Cook over a medium heat until the mixture is reduced by half.

Remove from heat and fold in the sour cream with a wooden spoon. Season with salt and freshly ground black pepper.

Serve warm with toasted bread, roast beef, trout or smoked salmon.

Fried Bread
(only) $ 1.00
ried Bread with
Toppings: Cream
Strawberry $ 1.50
Passion fruit
Golden Syrup
ied Bread with
Mince Stew. $ 3.00
1aori Hamburgers $ 3.50
ied Bread with $ 3.00
curry
ea and Coffee $ 1.00

EXCLUSIVE

two | nibbly bits

BLUE CHEESE AND RASPBERRY TARTS

Prep 15 minutes
Makes 12

12 slices white sandwich bread
2 tablespoons liquid honey
oil spray
2 cups blue cheese, diced into chunks
2 punnets fresh raspberries

Preheat the oven to 200°C. Lightly spray muffin tins with oil.

Lay out the sliced bread on a flat surface. Cut off the crusts and paint the bread with honey. Press the bread down into the muffin tins, honey side up.

Bake for 10 minutes until the bread is golden brown. Allow to cool for 5 minutes on a rack. Spoon a little blue cheese and raspberries into each bread tart case. Serve straight away.

Wash raspberries before using, which should be within 1–3 days of purchase. Soft, watery fruit means the berries are overripe, while wrinkled fruit means they have been stored too long.

CHEESY SCONES

Prep 30 minutes
Makes 12

50g butter at room temperature, diced
1½ cups white flour, sifted
pinch salt
1 tablespoon baking powder
½ cup cheddar cheese, grated
1 teaspoon mustard powder
2 teaspoons fresh thyme, chopped
½ teaspoon cayenne pepper
¾ cup milk

Preheat the oven to 200°C. In a large bowl rub the butter into the sifted flour, then add the salt and baking powder.

Add two-thirds of the grated cheese and then the

mustard, thyme and cayenne. Gradually cut the milk (you might not need it all) into the flour mix with a knife until you have a nice soft dough.

Roll the dough out to 2 centimetres thick, then cut out scones with a small floured glass. Place the scones on a buttered baking tray, sprinkle with the remaining cheese and bake for 12–15 minutes.

Cool on a wire rack for 5 minutes, then eat warm with my nectarine butter on page 18.

There is an endless variation of scones you can make, limited only by your imagination: pesto, roast pepper, Parmesan cheese, blue cheese, buttermilk, roast tomato, olive or even chocolate.

MUSHROOMS STUFFED WITH BACON

Prep 20 minutes
Makes 12

12 fresh button mushrooms
1 tablespoon olive oil
6 lean bacon rashers
½ cup cream cheese
3 tablespoons sour cream
1 spring onion, finely chopped
2 teaspoons garlic powder
1 tablespoon fresh thyme, finely chopped
salt and freshly ground black pepper to taste

Heat your barbecue to a medium temperature.

Remove the stems from the mushrooms and gently wash the caps.

Paint the mushrooms with olive oil and cook for 1½ minutes each side on the barbecue. Set aside. At the same time, cook the bacon until crispy, then finely chop.

In a bowl mix the bacon, cream cheese, sour cream, spring onion, garlic and thyme and season with salt and pepper.

Spoon the bacon and cheese mixture into each mushroom cap. ▸

Do not overcook the mushrooms on the barbecue or they will become difficult to fill. The mushrooms could also be cooked in an oven or a pan.

Try barbecuing some watercress and adding it to the cheese mixture. Grilling watercress mellows that mustardy bite.

STUFFING TO NIBBLE ON
Prep 20 minutes
Serves 4

2 tablespoons olive oil
1 onion, finely chopped
3 medium potatoes, peeled and cut into small dice
4 cloves garlic, peeled and halved
1 tablespoon fresh thyme, finely chopped
1 tablespoon rosemary, chopped
8 black olives, pitted
8 green olives, pitted
1 cup fresh breadcrumbs, chunky style
2 cups rocket leaves, chopped
zest of 1 lemon, finely chopped
salt and freshly ground black pepper to taste

In a frying pan over medium heat add the oil, chopped onion, potato and garlic and sauté for about 5 minutes until soft.

Add the herbs and olives, stirring with a wooden spoon. Then add the breadcrumbs and continue cooking until they are crisply golden and coating the potatoes.

Test the potatoes with a small knife; they should hold their shape but be cooked through.

Finally, add the rocket and cook for a few seconds. Take the pan off the heat, add the lemon zest, then season with salt and freshly ground black pepper.

Serve as a snack on a small plate with smoked salmon or prosciutto. This potato dish also makes a tasty addition to any main meat or seafood dish.

COCONUT FRITTERS
Prep 30 minutes
Makes 12

1 cup pumpkin, peeled and grated
1 medium-sized potato, peeled and grated
1 small onion, finely chopped
1/2 cup desiccated coconut
1 heaped tablespoon minced ginger
1 fresh chilli, seeded and finely chopped
1 tablespoon curry powder
2 teaspoons salt
1 large egg
2 cups white flour
2 teaspoons baking powder
vegetable oil for frying (500mls peanut oil)

In a large bowl mix the pumpkin, potato, onion, coconut, ginger, chilli, curry powder, salt and egg with a wooden spoon until combined.

Fold in the flour and baking powder and continue mixing until fully incorporated.

Shape the mixture with your hands into golf ball-sized patties.

Heat oil to 180°C in a deep saucepan. Check the temperature with a candy thermometer.

Carefully slip some of the patties into the hot oil, being careful not to overcrowd the pan. Fry for about 3 minutes on each side until golden brown, turning once.

Using a slotted spoon, carefully transfer the patties to paper towels to drain. Repeat with the remaining patties. Serve warm with sour cream flavoured with minced sun-dried tomatoes.

When deep-frying be very careful and do not leave the heating pot unattended. Test the temperature of the oil as it heats with little bits of fritter batter. Never allow the oil to go to a blue smoke stage or above 180°C.

mushrooms stuffed with bacon

banana pikelets with fruit salad

BANANA PIKELETS WITH FRUIT SALAD

Prep 30 minutes
Makes 12 pikelets

6 apricots, stoned and diced
3 cups watermelon, diced
juice of 2 limes
½ cup orange juice
1 teaspoon baking powder
½ teaspoon salt
1½ cups flour
1 teaspoon baking soda
1 egg
½ cup white sugar
1 banana, peeled and mashed
¾ cup milk
1 tablespoon butter, melted
oil spray

In a bowl mix together the apricots, watermelon, lime juice and orange juice, cover and chill in the refrigerator.

Into a large bowl sift the baking powder, salt, flour and baking soda.

In a separate bowl beat the egg and sugar together, then stir in the mashed banana.

Beat the sifted ingredients and milk alternately into the egg mixture. Lastly fold the melted butter into the batter.

Heat a large pan and lightly spray with oil. Drop a tablespoonful of batter into the pan, and wait for bubbles to form and break on the surface before turning. Keep cooked pikelets warm under a tea towel.

Serve with the chilled fruit salad.

A variation on this fruit salad uses pineapple. When buying a fresh pineapple always select one that feels heavy. Pull one of its leaves, and if it comes off easily then the pineapple should be ripe.

CORNMEAL PANCAKES WITH PLUMS

Prep 30 minutes
Makes 12

1 cup fine cornmeal
½ cup white flour
½ teaspoon salt
2 tablespoons sugar
2 teaspoons baking powder
½ teaspoon baking soda
2 whole eggs
1¼ cups buttermilk
2 tablespoons melted butter
oil spray
6 plums, stoned and quartered
6 bacon rashers, cooked (keep warm)
maple syrup

Sift the dry ingredients into a large bowl.

In another bowl beat the eggs, buttermilk and melted butter.

Add the wet ingredients to the dry cornmeal mix and beat to a smooth batter.

Let the batter stand for 10 minutes. Heat a large frying pan over a medium temperature and spray with oil.

Use a tablespoon to drop a large spoonful of the batter into the pan. Cook the pancake until golden brown on each side, turning once. Repeat this process until all the batter is used up. Serve the pancakes with the bacon, plums and maple syrup.

These pancakes are made with fine cornmeal, not the course grit-like variety. Try them as an accompaniment to roast chicken and my mushroom sauce (see page 25).

cornmeal pancakes with plums

AVOCADO WITH PINENUTS

Prep 10 minutes
Makes 3 cups

3 avocados, peeled and seeded
juice of 1 lemon
4 cloves garlic, peeled and minced
1 tablespoon olive oil
¼ cup plain yoghurt
½ teaspoon sweet paprika
salt and freshly ground black pepper to taste
1 tablespoon pinenuts

Place 2½ avocados in a food processor, keeping ½ aside to garnish your dip. Add the lemon juice, garlic and oil and process until smooth.

Add the yoghurt and paprika and mix until the ingredients are completely incorporated.

Season with salt and pepper to taste. Scrape the mixture into a serving bowl and garnish with the remaining chopped avocado.

In a small pan over medium heat sauté the pinenuts for 2 minutes until golden brown. Sprinkle the nuts on top of the avocado. Serve your dip with sliced bagel or vegetable crudités.

To remove an avocado stone, cut around the whole avocado lengthwise, then take it in both hands and twist it apart. The seed will remain in one of the halves. Now chop into the stone with the blade of a large knife hard enough for the blade to become lodged in it. Holding the fruit firmly, twist the knife. You should be able to pull the seed out with the knife still attached.

BALSAMIC-FLAVOURED OLIVES AND ONIONS

Prep 10 minutes plus overnight marinating
Makes enough for 8

¼ cup good quality balsamic vinegar
4 tablespoons olive oil
1 tablespoon maple syrup
1 tablespoon fresh oregano, finely chopped
½ cup Italian parsley, finely chopped
2 cloves garlic, minced
½ teaspoon Maldon sea salt
freshly ground black pepper to taste
1 cup canned artichoke hearts, drained and quartered
1 cup Kalamata olives, pitted if possible
1 cup small pickled onions

In a large bowl whisk together the vinegar, oil, maple syrup, oregano, parsley, garlic, salt and pepper.

Add the artichoke hearts, olives and onions and gently toss to coat.

Cover and refrigerate overnight. Bring to room temperature before serving. Serve with a bowl of freshly made bread croutons tossed in grated Parmesan.

Good quality balsamic vinegar and real maple syrup make this recipe work. Once you've tried real maple syrup you will never go back to the imitation stuff. When choosing, remember good maple syrup is graded by colour; the lighter the colour, the higher the grade. Two brands to look out for are Cedarvale or pure Vermont.

balsamic-flavoured olives and onions

three | cool drinks

d's pineapple twister

D'S PINEAPPLE TWISTER

Prep 10 minutes
Makes 8 drinks

2 cups fresh grapefruit juice
2 cups fresh orange juice
1/4 cup lime juice
1 pineapple, peeled, cored and chopped (about 4 cups)
2 cups rum

Put the grapefruit juice, orange juice, lime juice, pineapple and rum into a blender and pulse until smooth. Depending on the size of your blender you may need to do this in two batches.

Pour the twister into a large jug and refrigerate, making sure you cover the jug.

This drink can be made a day ahead, but remember to stir the cocktail before serving. Drop the rum out of the recipe if you are after an alcohol-free twister.

This is a recipe I picked up in the Caribbean while working on a motor yacht. Make sure you pick a ripe, tropical-smelling pineapple for a refreshing, tropical-tasting drink.

GINGER LEMONADE

Prep 30 minutes plus chilling
Makes 4 drinks

1/2 cup fresh mint leaves, chopped
4 heaped tablespoons fresh ginger, unpeeled and diced
1/3 cup maple syrup
4 cups boiling water
1/2 cup fresh lemon juice
lime slices
orange slices
ice cubes

Put the chopped mint, ginger and maple syrup into a bowl, then pour over the boiling water.

Let the liquid steep for 30 minutes before straining into another bowl, squeezing the ginger to extract all the liquid. Add the lemon juice and taste test for sweetness.

Cover and refrigerate until cold. Fill glasses with ice cubes. Pour over the lemonade and garnish with citrus slices.

For something a little different, try using 4 stalks of fresh lemongrass instead of the mint. Coarsely chop and mash with a rolling pin to release the flavour.

NOEMI'S RICE COOLER

Prep 30 minutes plus standing and chilling
Makes 6 drinks

1 cup rice (jasmine or basmati)
8 cups water
1 cinnamon stick, broken up
white sugar to taste, begin with 1/2 cup

Put all the ingredients into a large bowl and leave for 3 hours at room temperature.

Place a pot on low heat, add the ingredients from the bowl and simmer gently for 30 minutes.

Transfer cooked rice mix to a blender and pulse energetically before straining through a muslin cloth or clean dampened tea towel.

Taste for sweetness and add more sugar if necessary. Chill for a couple of hours. Before pouring give it a good stir, then serve over crushed ice.

The recipe comes courtesy of my favourite El Salvadoran, Noemi. The rice tends to settle on the bottom, so use a straw to stir and suck. You can make a couple of different variations by adding fresh, blended strawberries or melted chocolate.

noemi's rice cooler

sangria cha cha

spiced tomato cocktail

ALMOND SILK
Prep 15 minutes
4 servings

3 cups water
1 cup blanched almonds
4 tablespoons sunflower seeds
10 black peppercorns
2 cups milk
½ cup sugar
1 teaspoon rose water

Put half the water, almonds, sunflower seeds and peppercorns in a food processor or blender and blend at high speed until finely ground.

Strain the liquid into a jug through a muslin cloth or fine sieve.

Return the ground almond mixture left in the cloth to the blender and add the remaining 1½ cups of water. Blend again and strain the liquid once more into the jug. ▶

Throw away the ground nut mix.

Add the milk, sugar and rose water to the almond water in the jug and give it a good stir. Taste for sweetness.

Chill the drink and stir well before serving with crushed ice in small cups.

SANGRIA CHA CHA
Prep 10 minutes plus chilling
Makes 10 drinks

¼ **cup white sugar**
1 **cup water**
3 **limes, thinly sliced**
2 **lemons, thinly sliced**
2 **oranges, thinly sliced**
1 **bottle dry white wine**
1 **bottle red wine**
3 **cups ginger ale**

In a large bowl dissolve the sugar in the water, then add the sliced fruit, white wine and red wine.

Place the covered sangria in the refrigerator and allow at least 4 hours for the fruit to infuse into the wine. For even better flavour, leave overnight.

Add the ginger ale just before serving. Pour the sangria into a ceramic pitcher filled with ice and serve at once.

Some recipes for sangria finish off with brandy. I worked in Serville, Spain, for 6 months and had many an encounter with this version. I found it finished me off well and truly!

LIME MARGARITAS
Prep 10 minutes
Makes 4 drinks

1 **cup tequila**
¼ **cup Cointreau (orange liqueur)**
¼ **cup fresh lime juice**

1 **teaspoon sugar**
12 **large ice cubes**
crushed rock salt
lime slices

Put the Tequila, Cointreau, lime juice, sugar and ice in a blender.

Pulse until slushy, then taste test for sweetness.

Moisten the lip of each margarita glass with a lime and dip in the salt, rotating to make sure you cover the entire rim.

Serve with a slice of lime. If you find lime a bit sharp, add a peeled and chopped mango to the mix before blending.

SPICED TOMATO COCKTAIL
Prep 10 minutes
Makes 6 drinks

⅓ **cup fresh lime juice**
3 **chilli peppers, stemmed and seeded**
1 **cup coriander, stemmed and chopped**
6 **cups tomato juice**
1 **cup tequila**
salt and freshly ground coarse black pepper to taste

In a blender mix the lime juice, chilli peppers and coriander.

Pour in the tomato juice and tequila and blend again. Strain the cocktail into a jug.

Serve this drink over ice, garnished with freshly ground coarse black pepper and salt to taste. Great at breakfast, lunch or dinner!

lime margaritas

apple punch

◄ strawberry daiquiri
bananarama ▼

APPLE PUNCH

Prep 10 minutes plus freezing
Makes 10 drinks

2 cups apple juice
½ cup white sugar
2 cups applesauce (naturally sweetened)
2 cups real orange juice
juice of 2 lemons
1 teaspoon red food colouring
5 cups premium-brand lemonade

In a saucepan over medium heat add the apple juice and sugar and stir until dissolved.

Remove from the heat and stir in the applesauce, orange juice, lemon juice and red food colouring. Transfer to a bowl and cool completely.

Place in a covered container and freeze for about 5 hours until firm.

To serve this drink, soften the frozen apple punch at room temperature for about 10 minutes.

With a large spoon scrape a portion into a punch cup and fill with lemonade.

There is no alcohol in this drink, but at this stage you could add a splash of vodka or tequila, or replace the lemonade with sparkling wine.

STRAWBERRY DAIQUIRI

Prep 10 minutes
Makes 2 drinks

½ cup dark rum
½ cup Cointreau (orange liqueur)
1 punnet strawberries, hulled (2 cups)
1 tablespoon white sugar
juice of 2 limes
10 ice cubes

To hull strawberries, use a sturdy plastic straw. Push it up through the bottom of the strawberry and through the top.

Put all the ingredients into a food processor or blender and pulse to a slush.

Pour into tall, chilled glasses.

Enjoy too many of these and the evening will creep up on you faster than you realise! Another of my favourite daiquiri flavours is peach. Stone super ripe peaches, freeze the peach quarters and use peach schnapps instead of Cointreau.

BANANARAMA

Prep 5 minutes
Makes 4 drinks

4 small ripe bananas, peeled and chopped
2 cups vanilla ice-cream
1 cup white rum
2½ cups milk

Place all the ingredients into a food processor or blender and pulse to a thick cream.

Check the consistency. If the drink is too thick to suck up a straw, add a little more rum to thin it down. If you like the taste of coffee, a ½ cup of Kahlua makes a nice addition to this drink.

After bananas have ripened, store them in the refrigerator to slow down further ripening. The skin will turn dark brown, but this does not damage the fruit inside. If bananas become too ripe then freeze them in their skins.

four | from the sea

scallops with whisky and bacon

SCALLOPS WITH WHISKY AND BACON
Prep 20 minutes
Serves 4

4 rashers bacon
3 tablespoons vegetable oil
24 scallops with roe on
¼ cup whisky
juice of 1 lemon
4 tablespoons crème fraîche
salt and freshly ground black pepper to taste
1 large fresh mango, skinned, stone removed and sliced

Preheat the oven to 180°C. Arrange the bacon slices on a baking sheet and bake for about 8 minutes until golden. Cut each rasher into strips and set aside.

Add the oil to a large pan and heat to a medium temperature. Add the scallops and sear for about 1½ minutes per side. Do not overcook. The cooked scallops should be light brown but still soft to the touch. Transfer them to a plate, leaving the cooking juices in the pan.

Remove the pan from the heat and add the whisky and lemon juice. Set the whisky mixture alight to burn off the alcohol. After the flames die out, whisk in the crème fraîche over a low heat.

Return the scallops to the sauce, including any juices that have gathered on the plate. Season with salt and pepper to taste and warm for 1 minute. Serve immediately with the strips of bacon and slices of fresh mango, drizzling the sauce around the scallops.

If you're not comfortable flambéing the whisky, you can just simmer it until the alcohol burns off. Too much seafood in the pan at one time will bring down the cooking temperature and also make it difficult to turn the seafood over.

GRILLED SNAPPER WITH RED GRAPEFRUIT

Prep 30 minutes
Serves 4

2 cobs of fresh corn, kernels cut off
2 ripe nectarines, stoned and diced
1 red pepper, diced
1 red onion, peeled and diced
1 tablespoon fresh basil, diced
2 tablespoons vegetable oil
2 tablespoons maple syrup
2 tablespoons Dijon mustard
2 tablespoons white wine vinegar
salt and freshly ground black pepper to taste
1 cup buttermilk
1 tablespoon tobasco sauce
1 cup fine cornmeal
½ cup white flour
salt and freshly ground black pepper to taste
4 red snapper fillets
1 tablespoon vegetable oil
1 ruby red grapefruit, peeled and sliced into rings

In a large bowl combine the corn, nectarines, pepper, onion and basil and set aside.

In a small saucepan over medium heat bring the oil, maple syrup, mustard and vinegar to a simmer.

Remove the pan from the heat and pour the warm vinaigrette over the vegetable mixture, tossing to coat. Season with salt and pepper and set aside.

In a bowl stir together the buttermilk and tobasco sauce. Mix the flour with the cornmeal and salt and pepper and pour onto a large plate.

Dip the snapper fillets in the buttermilk and coat evenly in the flour mixture.

Heat a large frying pan to a medium temperature and add a tablespoon of oil. Pan-fry the fish for 4 minutes on each side, turning carefully.

Serve the snapper with the corn sauce and a slice of grapefruit.

Meaty fillets like grouper and snapper need a little more care. These fillets are usually about 3cm thick and cook quickly. They are best grilled directly over medium to high heat so you get a crusty outside and juicy centre.

PRAWNS WITH FRESH PINEAPPLE

Prep 20 minutes
Serves 4

½ cup coconut cream
2 tablespoons red curry paste
2 cups coconut milk
½ cup fresh basil leaves
½ fresh pineapple, peeled, cored and cut into wedges
1 tablespoon brown sugar
1 chilli, seeded and sliced
3 kaffir lime leaves, fresh or dried
500 grams prawns, deveined (about 24)

In a saucepan over medium heat add the coconut cream and bring to a simmer. Add the curry paste, stir until sauce is blended and cook for 2 minutes.

Now add the coconut milk, basil, pineapple, sugar, chilli and lime leaves, stirring until the sauce comes to the boil.

Reduce heat to a low simmer and cook gently for 5 minutes. Add the prawns and cook for 2–3 minutes. Serve with steamed basmati rice.

Coconut cream settles at the top of canned coconut milk. Be careful not to shake the can before opening, then you can remove the cream with a spoon.

grilled snapper with red grapefruit

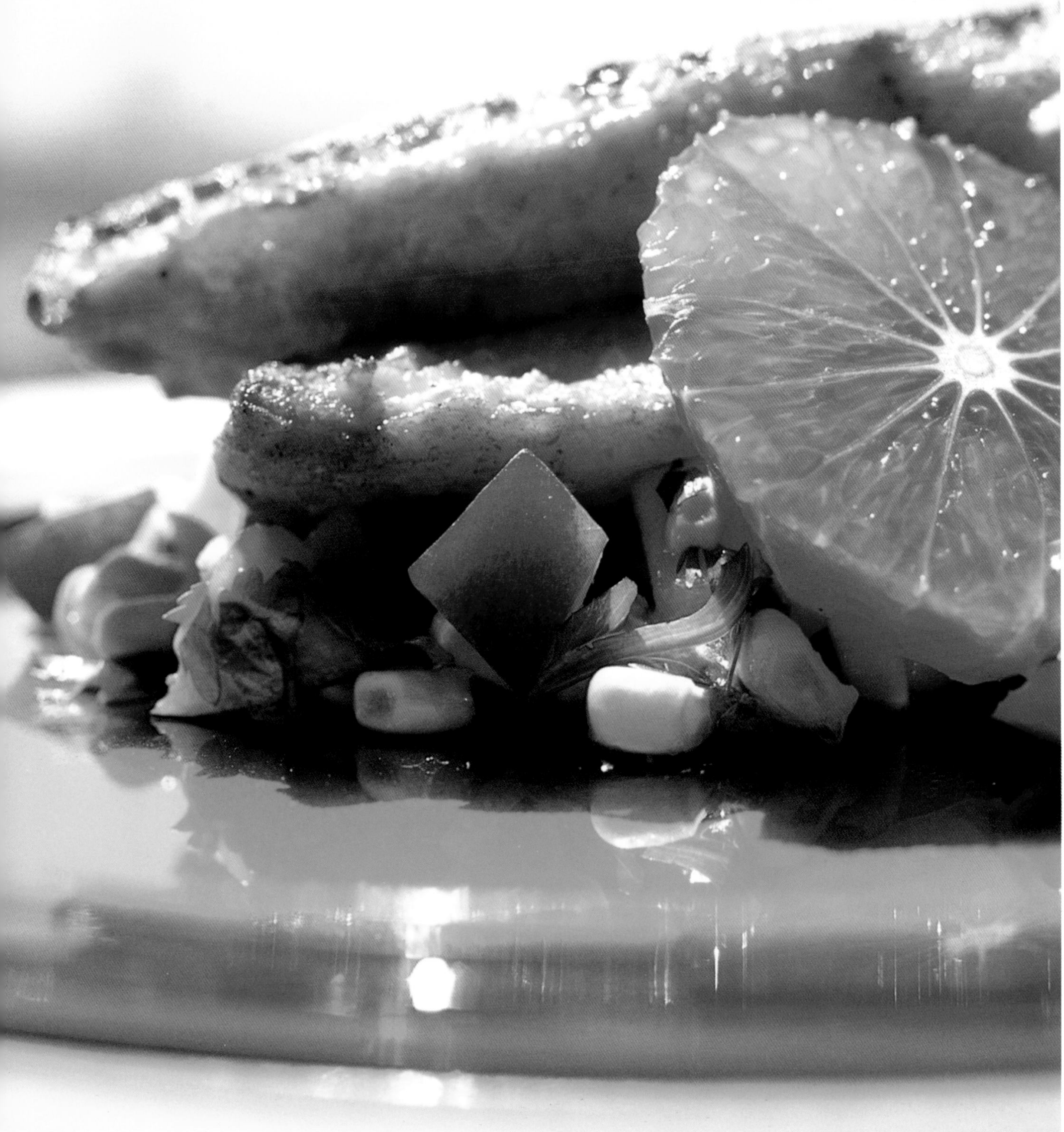

CHILLED MUSSELS WITH HORSERADISH

Prep 20 minutes plus 4 hours chilling
Serves 4

400 grams smoked fish, snapper or salmon
375 grams marinated mussels, drained
1 small red onion, peeled and diced
1 yellow pepper, diced
2 sticks celery, washed and diced
3 tablespoons olive oil
2 tablespoons red wine vinegar
2 tablespoons horseradish sauce
1 tablespoon liquid honey
juice of 1 lemon
2 tablespoons chives, minced
salt and white pepper to taste

Remove any skin or fish bones from the smoked fish. Cut into large dice and place in a bowl with the drained marinated mussels.

Now add the red onion, yellow pepper, celery, olive oil, vinegar, horseradish, honey, lemon and chives and season with salt and pepper.

Cover the bowl and chill in the refrigerator for 4 hours. Serve the chilled seafood salad with fresh bread to dunk in the vinaigrette.

I based the idea for this recipe on a dish my Dad would make every Christmas or birthday. My father was a crayfisherman, so he made his version with freshly cooked crayfish. Looking back we were pretty spoiled as kids. I grew up thinking every family ate crayfish a couple of times a week!

MUSSELS IN GARLIC CURRY

Prep 20 minutes
Serves 4

32 Greenshell mussels, cleaned
1 cup white wine
1 tablespoon butter
1 small onion, peeled and finely chopped
3 cloves garlic, finely chopped
1 tablespoon white flour
2 teaspoons curry powder
pinch saffron
½ teaspoon celery salt
2 tablespoons brandy
1 cup coconut cream
salt and freshly ground black pepper to taste
2 tablespoons fresh coriander, chopped

In a pan over medium heat, add the mussels and wine, cover, and cook until the shellfish open.

To save all the mussel juice, pour the cooked mussels into a colander over a bowl. Keep the mussels warm.

Melt the butter in a saucepan over medium heat. Add the onion, garlic, flour, curry powder, saffron and celery salt and cook gently for 3 minutes.

Add the brandy, mussel juice and coconut cream and bring the sauce to a simmer. Taste for seasoning.

Arrange the cooked mussels in bowls, pouring the sauce over them. Scatter with coriander and serve with toasted baguettes.

Fresh mussels should smell like sweet salt water, as if they are just out of the ocean. If they smell fishy, don't buy them. Mussels love the cold, so if you don't use them right away, store them on ice.

CRAB WITH POTATO AND GRUYÈRE

Prep 30 minutes plus 70 minutes baking potatoes
Serves 4

4 large baked potatoes
3 tablespoons butter
½ cup onion, finely chopped
½ cup mushrooms, sliced
2 cups crabmeat, canned or frozen
1 cup white wine
2 tablespoons yoghurt
2 tablespoons sour cream
¾ cup Gruyère cheese, grated
freshly ground black pepper

Cut the baked potatoes in half, lengthwise. Spoon the potato flesh out, mash in a bowl and set aside. Reserve the potato skin shells.

In a pan over medium heat, melt the butter and sauté the onion for 5 minutes. Add the sliced mushrooms and sauté for 5 minutes more.

Add the crabmeat and wine and simmer gently, stirring with a wooden spoon until the liquid is absorbed.

Remove from the heat and stir in the yoghurt and sour cream.

Add the onion and crabmeat mixture to the mashed potato together with ½ the Gruyère cheese. Mix together with a spoon and season with pepper.

Mould the crab mixture into the potato skins. Sprinkle with the remaining cheese and bake at 180°C until the cheese bubbles. Make sure you bake your potatoes slowly – they should take about 70 minutes at 180°C.

The crabmeat in this recipe can easily be replaced with any cooked white fish or smoked salmon trimmings. For a stronger flavour use Havarti cheese instead of Gruyère.

TUNA WITH ARTICHOKES AND TOMATO

Prep 40 minutes
Serves 4

¼ cup olive oil
2 garlic cloves, peeled and minced
1 large onion, peeled and thinly sliced
6 small artichoke hearts, drained (450 gram can)
4 tomatoes, cored and quartered
3 tablespoons parsley, chopped
1 tablespoon fresh thyme, finely chopped
salt and freshly ground black pepper to taste
800 grams tuna, trimmed and cut into steaks
1 tablespoon olive oil
juice of 1 lemon

Place a heavy frying pan on low heat, add ¼ cup olive oil, garlic and onion and cook for 10 minutes until soft and translucent.

Cut the artichokes into halves, add to the pan together with the tomatoes and cook for a further 5 minutes, stirring occasionally.

Take the pan off the heat, add the parsley and thyme, season with salt and pepper and set aside.

Season the tuna with salt and pepper. Place a grill pan over a high heat and add a tablespoon of olive oil to the pan.

Cook the tuna for about 2 minutes on each side. Serve the fish on the onion and artichoke sauce with a squeeze of lemon juice to finish.

If you roll a lemon firmly against the bench-top under the palm of your hand, you get twice as much juice out of it, as the rolling breaks the juice sacks inside the fruit.

smoked salmon with egg and chives

SMOKED SALMON WITH EGG AND CHIVES

Prep 20 minutes
Makes 8

4 whole eggs
1 loaf tomato bread, or use sourdough bread
¼ cup sour cream
400 grams smoked salmon, sliced
3 tablespoons chives, minced
salt and freshly ground black pepper to taste

Place the eggs in a single layer in a pot to cook evenly. Cover with cold water then place on a high heat, stirring occasionally.

Cook 3 minutes for a soft-boiled egg. Plunge the eggs into cold water for 30 seconds and peel. Carefully cut the eggs in half with a very sharp knife.

Cut the tomato bread into 8 slices and spread with sour cream. Spoon on the smoked salmon and sprinkle with minced chives. Top the salmon with ½ a boiled egg and season with salt and pepper.

To serve as finger food, make sure you buy a loaf similar in shape to a baguette.

My favourite toy in the kitchen is my eggrite eggtimer. This is a timer you place in the water with the eggs and it shows you exactly when the egg is cooked just the way you want it.

SWORDFISH WITH ALMOND SAUCE

Prep 20 minutes plus 2 hours marinating
Serves 4

800 grams swordfish, cut into 4cm thick steaks
salt and freshly ground black pepper
2 tablespoons olive oil
1 tablespoon fresh oregano, chopped
juice of 1 lemon
3 tablespoons olive oil
¼ cup blanched almond slivers
2 cloves garlic, peeled and minced
3 red peppers, roasted, skinned and seeded
½ teaspoon salt
pinch cayenne pepper
2 teaspoons sherry vinegar

Season the swordfish with a little salt and pepper, then marinate with the oil, chopped oregano and lemon juice for 2 hours, covered in the refrigerator.

Heat a small pan over a medium heat, add the oil and toast the almonds until golden brown. Spoon both the almonds and the oil into a bowl to cool.

Put the garlic, peppers, almonds and oil into a blender. Season with salt, cayenne pepper and sherry vinegar and process to a smooth paste. Set aside.

Heat a barbecue or stovetop grill pan to a medium heat.

Grill the swordfish for 3 minutes on each side, turning only once. Swordfish should not be overcooked as it is very low in fat and dries out easily.

Serve immediately on warm plates with a dollop of the almond sauce.

Don't even think about putting the fish on the grill until it is hot. Remember that nothing causes a piece of fish to stick more than putting it on a lukewarm surface.

COCKLES AND CHORIZO SAUSAGE

Prep 30 minutes
Serves 4

20 live cockles, scrubbed
2 tablespoons fine yellow cornmeal
500 grams dried spaghetti
2 teaspoons vegetable oil
1 onion, peeled and chopped
4 chorizo sausages, sliced into rings
1 can tomatoes, chopped
½ cup water
¼ cup Italian parsley, chopped
salt and freshly ground black pepper to taste

Place the cockles in a bowl, cover with water and sprinkle over the cornmeal. Leave in the refrigerator for at least 2 hours or overnight.

Bring a large pot of salted water to the boil, add the pasta and cook for 8 minutes. Strain into a colander and run under cold water. Set aside.

Heat the oil in a large pan, add the onion and sauté for about 3 minutes. Add the chorizo and cook for a further 2 minutes, stirring often until the sausage is lightly browned. Add the tomatoes and their juice to the chorizo and simmer gently for 5 minutes.

Add ½ cup water to the chorizo, then add the cockles and steam for about 8 minutes until they open. Discard any clams that do not open.

Grab 4 large handfuls of the cooked spaghetti and add to the pot with the cockles. Stir gently and sprinkle on the parsley. Season with salt and freshly ground black pepper. Serve immediately.

Adding cornmeal to the cockle-soaking water helps the bivalves open up and release any sand locked in their shells. Make sure you use fine yellow cornmeal. Don't use cornflour or your cockles will end up with a glue stuffing.

five Super Salads

fennel bulb with mushrooms and parmesan

FENNEL BULB WITH MUSHROOMS AND PARMESAN

Prep 20 minutes
Serves 4

4 small fennel bulbs, trimmed and cut into thin slices
2 large red bell peppers, seeded and cut into strips
8 mushrooms, wiped and thinly sliced
¼ cup shaved Parmesan
¼ cup lemon juice
3 tablespoons sherry vinegar
1 clove garlic, peeled and minced
2 tablespoons Italian parsley, finely chopped
2 tablespoons chives, chopped
½ cup olive oil
salt and freshly ground black pepper to taste

In a large salad bowl combine the fennel, bell peppers, mushrooms and Parmesan.

Whisk together the lemon juice, sherry vinegar, garlic, parsley, chives, oil and salt and pepper. Toss with the salad and serve.

This salad would be the perfect accompaniment to a fish dish. Fennel bulb has a tangy, liquorice flavour. I find the smaller bulbs are more tender and not as woody as their big brothers.

GRILLED CAESAR SALAD

Prep 90 minutes
Serves 4

3 large tomatoes, cored and diced
1 red onion, peeled and diced
2 tablespoons coriander, finely chopped
juice of 1 lime
salt to taste
½ cup toasted pumpkin seeds
1½ teaspoons ground cumin
½ teaspoon chilli powder
2 tablespoons canned anchovies, drained
1 tablespoon Dijon mustard
2 cloves garlic, minced
1 tablespoon Worcestershire sauce
¼ cup red wine vinegar
¼ teaspoon pepper
1 teaspoon tobasco sauce
½ cup olive oil
4 hearts Cos (Romaine) lettuces cut in half lengthwise

Put the tomatoes, onion, coriander, lime juice and salt into a bowl. Mix together, cover and chill for 1 hour.

In a small bowl mix the pumpkin seeds, cumin and chilli powder until the seeds are well coated. Set aside.

To make the Caesar dressing, combine the anchovies, Dijon mustard, garlic, Worcestershire sauce, wine vinegar and tobasco sauce in a blender. As you blend, gradually add the oil in a thin stream until the mixture becomes mayonnaise-like in consistency. Season to taste.

Heat barbecue or a frying pan to medium heat. Brush the lettuce halves with some of the Caesar dressing. Place face-down on the grill for 60 seconds or until seared. Remove to a plate.

Spoon the chilled tomato salsa onto each plate, arranging the lettuce leaves face-up on top. Paint with more dressing and scatter the spiced pumpkin seeds over the lettuce.

Salad greens will keep crisp for several days if rolled in absorbent towelling, popped into a zip-lock plastic bag and stored in the refrigerator. I have managed to keep salad greens for up to 2 weeks on motor yachts in remote locations using this method.

barbecued veges with capers

BARBECUED VEGES WITH CAPERS

Prep 40 minutes
Serves 4

1 eggplant, cut into rings
2 small fennel bulbs, cut into slices lengthwise
3 small zucchini, cut into strips
2 red onions, peeled and cut into rings
8 cherry tomatoes, cut in half
2 tablespoons fresh rosemary, finely chopped
2 tablespoons fresh thyme, finely chopped
1 teaspoon salt
1 teaspoon freshly ground black pepper
4 tablespoons olive oil
2 tablespoons capers

Place the vegetables in a baking dish. In a small bowl mix together the rosemary, thyme, salt, pepper and olive oil.

Sprinkle the herb marinade over the vegetables in the tray, toss well to coat and leave marinating for 20 minutes, turning from time to time.

Heat the barbecue to a medium temperature.

Place the marinated vegetables on a well-oiled grill and cook for about 6–8 minutes per side. Cooked, they should be lightly browned on the outside, tender and moist on the inside. Different vegetables cook at different speeds, so keep an eye on them and remove them as they are done.

Serve the grilled veges warm with the capers and a little of the herb marinade drizzled over the top.

Assume that most vegetables will need 1¹/₂ times the cooking time when prepared outdoors as compared to indoors. The only way to know for certain is to experiment with your grill. And try barbecuing other veges such as peppers, mushrooms, asparagus and avocados.

STRAWBERRY AND CAMEMBERT SALAD

Prep 20 minutes
Serves 4

1 large red onion, peeled and cut into wedges
1 tablespoon olive oil
4 heaped cups arugula leaves, washed
4 heaped cups baby spinach leaves, washed
12 strawberries, sliced
2 tablespoons olive oil
2 tablespoons balsamic vinegar
2 cups of Camembert cheese, cut into large dice
freshly ground black pepper

Heat a barbecue or grill pan to medium heat. Lightly brush onion wedges with oil and grill until tender, charring a little. Set aside.

Into a large bowl add the arugula, spinach, strawberries, olive oil, balsamic vinegar and grilled onion.

Toss gently with your hands until evenly coated, then divide equally between four bowls. Garnish with diced Camembert and season with pepper.

Strawberries are a good source of phytochemicals, nutrients that protect us against cancer, heart disease and ageing.

ASPARAGUS WITH TARRAGON

Prep 20 minutes
Serves 4

24 asparagus spears
¼ cup extra virgin olive oil
3 tablespoons fresh tarragon, finely chopped
3 tablespoons sherry vinegar
4 shallots, peeled and minced
½ teaspoon Maldon sea salt
freshly ground black pepper

Bring a pot of water to the boil. Cut off the woody ends of the asparagus and discard.

Plunge the asparagus into the boiling water until they turn bright green and are tender but not limp. This will take about 4 minutes.

Drain and pat dry, then place in a ceramic baking dish.

In a small bowl mix together the oil, tarragon, vinegar, shallots and salt and pepper. Pour this over the still warm asparagus – this is the secret to the dish. The tarragon sauce infuses into the asparagus, so leave it to steep for 5 minutes covered with a plate. Serve at room temperature.

If you use white asparagus it needs to be peeled before cooking. Eaten in its raw form it has a sweet nutty taste. The vinegar and tarragon combine well in this recipe – another fantastic taste combo to add to your repertoire.

TOMATO, LIME AND CORIANDER SALAD

Prep 20 minutes
Serves 4

1 clove garlic, peeled and minced
3 tablespoons coriander, finely chopped
3 tablespoons basil, finely chopped
1 tablespoon honey
zest of 1 lime, finely chopped
juice of 2 limes
¼ cup vegetable oil
½ teaspoon salt
6 vine-ripened tomatoes
8 cherry tomatoes
freshly ground black pepper

In a food processor add the garlic, coriander, basil, honey, zest, juice, oil and salt and pulse until smooth. Set aside. Alternatively, use a screw-top jar with a lid and shake for two minutes.

Thinly slice the two types of tomato and arrange together on plates. Grind some pepper on top of the tomatoes and spoon over the dressing.

Cover and chill for 10 minutes in the refrigerator before serving.

ASPARAGUS OMELETTE

Prep 40 minutes
Serves 10

12 asparagus spears
6 whole eggs
¼ cup Parmesan cheese, grated
2 tablespoons milk
salt to taste
½ teaspoon freshly ground black pepper
1 tablespoon butter
½ small onion, finely chopped
¼ cup Italian parsley, finely chopped
½ cup sour cream
3 tablespoons fresh chives, chopped

Heat the oven to 200°C. Cut the woody ends off the asparagus and cook in boiling water for 5 minutes. Remove and rinse under cold water to stop the cooking process, then cut into small rings. Pat dry and set aside.

In a large bowl whisk together the eggs, cheese, milk, salt and pepper.

In a medium-sized frying pan melt the butter over a moderate heat. Once the butter is foaming, add the onion and sauté for 2 minutes until soft.

Evenly sprinkle the asparagus and parsley over the bottom of the pan, then pour over the egg mixture. Reduce the heat to low and cook for 3–4 minutes, until the egg mixture is just firm around the edge.

Place the omelette in the oven and cook for 6–8 minutes until it is firmly set. Remove from the oven and turn out onto a plate. Cool on a rack for 10 minutes.

Cut the omelette into squares, arrange on a serving platter and garnish each square with a spoonful of sour cream and a sprinkle of chives.

This omelette cut into squares makes a great dish to take on picnics or out in the boat. Other versions I have made using the basic recipe are pickled onion, cooked potato, roasted eggplant or sautéed wood mushroom.

CHICK-PEA ONION RINGS

Prep 30 minutes
Serves 4

1 cup of yoghurt
1 spring onion, finely chopped
1 tablespoon ginger, peeled and finely chopped
1 tablespoon honey
¼ cup fresh mint leaves, chopped
1 cup coriander, finely chopped
salt and freshly ground black pepper to taste
1 cup chick-pea flour
1 cup warm water
1 teaspoon cayenne pepper
1 tablespoon ground cumin
2 tablespoons olive oil
3 large red onions, peeled and cut into thick, separate rings
4 cups peanut oil (for frying)

In a bowl whisk together the yoghurt, spring onion, ginger, honey, mint and coriander. Season to taste with salt and pepper. Set the sauce aside.

In another bowl combine the chick-pea flour with the water, cayenne pepper, cumin and olive oil and mix until smooth. Season to taste with salt.

Heat a deep fryer or pot of peanut oil to 180°C, checking the temperature with a candy thermometer. Dip the onion rings into the batter and coat evenly. Deep fry for 3–4 minutes until golden brown.

Remove the fried onions to a baking tray covered with paper towels and sprinkle with salt and pepper. Serve warm with the yoghurt sauce.

To store fresh coriander, pick out any wilted leaves and put the rest in a jar of water like a bunch of flowers. Cover the leaves with a plastic bag and put the whole thing in the refrigerator.

bean salad with cumin tofu

BEAN SALAD WITH CUMIN TOFU
Prep 20 minutes
Serves 4

1/3 cup sherry vinegar
2 tablespoons maple syrup
1 clove garlic, peeled and minced
2 teaspoons Dijon mustard
1/4 cup olive oil
4 cups cooked red kidney beans (2 cans drained)
2 red peppers, cored and diced
salt and freshly ground black pepper to taste
1/2 cup coriander, chopped
1 tablespoon ground cumin
2 cups silken tofu, diced
3 cups baby spinach, washed
1/4 cup pumpkin seeds, toasted

In a bowl whisk together the vinegar, maple syrup, garlic, mustard and olive oil until combined, then stir in the beans and red peppers. Season with salt and pepper and set aside.

Spread the coriander out on a plate, sprinkle on the cumin and roll the diced tofu in this herb spice mix, until evenly coated.

Arrange the spinach leaves on your serving plates, spoon the bean salad on top and scatter the herb-coated tofu around the beans.

I use silken tofu for this recipe because it absorbs flavour more easily than firm tofu and is better suited to salads. I eat a lot of tofu; it's one of the most important staples in my pantry.

SAFFRON RICE AND VERMICELLI
Prep 30 minutes
Serves 4

2 tablespoons olive oil
1/2 cup uncooked vermicelli (pasta), snapped into sticks
2 cups basmati rice, washed
4 cups chicken stock
1/4 teaspoon saffron threads
salt and freshly ground black pepper to taste
2 cups cooked canned beetroot, drained and cut into wedges
1/2 cup grated Parmesan cheese (optional)

In a saucepan on medium heat lightly fry the uncooked vermicelli in the olive oil as in a pilaf.

Add the rice and sauté for 2 minutes. Add enough chicken stock to cover the rice and pasta.

Bring the pasta and rice to the boil, then turn the heat down to low and add the saffron. Cover and cook gently for 10 minutes, stirring occasionally with a wooden spoon. Season with salt and freshly ground black pepper to taste.

Turn off the heat and let the dish sit covered for 5 minutes.

Fluff with a fork, then serve with the wedges of beetroot. You also have the option of enriching the dish with the grated Parmesan cheese.

Fresh saffron has a spicy honey smell and you only need a good pinch to colour and flavour most dishes. If you use too much it can make a dish taste bitter, and it is far too expensive to waste.

six | meat cookin'

steak with shiitake mushrooms and walnuts

STEAK WITH SHIITAKE MUSHROOMS AND WALNUTS

Prep 30 minutes
Serves 4

4 cups green beans, top and tailed
1 tablespoon butter
800 grams beef fillet, cut into 8 small steaks
salt and freshly ground black pepper to taste
1 tablespoon olive oil
12 fresh shiitake mushrooms, wiped clean
1 garlic clove, peeled and minced
1 tablespoon red wine vinegar
1 cup walnut pieces, lightly toasted

Preheat the oven to 190°C.

Bring a pot of water to the boil, cook the beans in the water for 4 minutes, drain well and set aside on a plate.

Heat an ovenproof pan over a high temperature, add the butter, then the seasoned steak. Sear the steak for a minute per side on both sides until browned. Transfer the steak to the oven, cook for 8 minutes for medium rare, or 11 minutes for medium. Rest on a warm plate for 5 minutes.

In a large pan over medium heat add the tablespoon of oil and sauté the garlic and mushrooms for about 4 minutes until lightly browned. Season with salt and pepper, then pour in the red wine vinegar.

Add the green beans and toss. Warm through for 1 minute and test for seasoning.

Serve the mushrooms and beans with the beef fillet, spooning the hot vinegar juice over the vegetables. Scatter over the walnuts to finish the dish.

Fresh green beans are one of the many joys of summer and if the beans are small and tender you might not even need to top and tail them. Feel the shiitake mushrooms to see how woody they are, as they may need to have the stems removed.

KIWI BURGERS

Prep 30 minutes
Serves 4

600 grams ground chuck steak
1 teaspoon salt
1 teaspoon freshly ground black pepper
4 hamburger buns, cut in half
1 tablespoon olive oil
4 canned or fresh pineapple rings
2 medium-sized beetroot, cut into slices
4 soft-boiled eggs, peeled and sliced
salt and freshly ground black pepper to taste
tomato sauce or mustard

Preheat the grill to medium-high.

Place the ground meat into a large bowl and sprinkle with salt and pepper. Using your hands, lightly mix meat to incorporate seasonings. Try not to overmix.

Divide mixture into 4 even piles. Shape into 4cm high meat patties. Don't compress the pattie but leave it loose.

Lightly oil grill. Place the meat patties on grill and cook for about 4 minutes per side for medium. When cooked, set aside on a plate and keep warm.

Brush inside of buns with olive oil. Place them oil side down on the grill and lightly toast for about 2 minutes. Repeat this process for the pineapple rings.

Assemble the burgers, burger bun, pineapple, meat pattie, sliced beetroot, sliced egg and tomato sauce as you like and season to taste.

The key to a good burger is the meat. Use fresh marbled beef and don't over-handle it. Make sure the salt is mixed through the meat, not just sprinkled on the top.

VENISON WITH ROCKET AND CHERRY TOMATOES

Prep 30 minutes
Serves 4

600 grams venison, Denver leg
salt and freshly ground black pepper
1 tablespoon oil
2 cups cherry tomatoes, cut in half
4 cups rocket, small leaves washed
I cup snow peas, top and tailed
2 limes cut in half
freshly ground white pepper

Preheat the oven to 200°C. Denver leg usually comes in a big chunk with smaller sub primals, so cut the large chunk in half lengthwise. The smaller your pieces of meat, the quicker they will cook.

Season the venison with salt and pepper. Heat a large ovenproof pan over a high temperature, add the oil and sear the meat for about 4 minutes, until dark brown all over.

Once the meat is nicely browned, place the pan in the oven to finish cooking. The venison will take another 5–6 minutes to cook. Venison is very lean, so don't overcook it. Give it a nick with your knife and check.

Remove the venison from the oven and let it rest for 5 minutes on a covered plate. Don't rest it in the hot pan or it will keep cooking.

Arrange the rocket, tomatoes and snow peas on 4 plates. Slice the venison across the grain and arrange on the vegetables. Squeeze lime on the salad and sprinkle freshly ground white pepper on the venison.

You can also serve this venison dish with my rhubarb sauce on page 21. Venison has come a long way from the strong gamey taste it once had; it now has a clean caramel flavour – definitely a lean food we should all be eating in the future.

venison with rocket and cherry tomatoes

macaroni and gruyère cheese

MACARONI AND GRUYÈRE CHEESE

Prep 20 minutes
Serves 4

2 cups macaroni pasta
2 tablespoons unsalted butter, softened
2 cups Gruyère cheese, grated
salt and white pepper to taste
1 tablespoon fresh thyme, chopped
8 ham slices, cut into strips

Bring a large pot of salted water to the boil. Drop in the macaroni elbows and cook according to instructions on the packet, usually 6–8 minutes. Drain and return to the same pot.

Add the butter and stir until melted. Add ½ of the cheese and stir again until melted.

Add the rest of the cheese, but don't overmix as you are after texture in this dish.

Season with salt and white pepper to taste. Serve in bowls scattered with chopped thyme. Top each bowl with a few strips of ham.

This is one of the original comfort foods. Its magic is the mouth texture of the elbow-shaped pasta, that silky sensation coming from the air trapped inside the elbow. Other tastes you might want to add to the dish are crispy buttered breadcrumbs on top, cayenne pepper or cheddar cheese.

BEEF STROGANOFF

Prep 30 minutes
Serves 4

1 tablespoon olive oil
2 cups button mushrooms, wiped clean and sliced
1 tablespoon olive oil
500 grams beef fillet, cut into 1 x 5cm strips
1 tablespoon unsalted butter
1 small onion, finely chopped (½ cup)
1 tablespoon tomato paste

1 tablespoon brown sugar
1 tablespoon flour
1 cup chicken stock
½ cup white wine
½ cup low-fat sour cream
salt and freshly ground black pepper to taste
400 grams noodles, cooked and tossed in oil
2 tablespoons parsley, chopped

Heat 1 tablespoon oil in a frying pan over medium-high heat until hot. Add mushrooms and cook over high heat for 30 seconds. Lower temperature and cook for about 4 minutes until mushrooms are lightly browned. Transfer to a bowl.

Return the pan to a high heat and add 1 tablespoon of oil. Place beef fillet strips in the pan. Using tongs, spread the meat into a single layer and cook for about 4 minutes until well browned. Season with salt and pepper, then transfer to a bowl with the mushrooms.

Return pan to medium heat and add butter. When butter melts, add the onion, tomato paste and brown sugar. Cook, stirring frequently, until onion is lightly browned, then stir in the flour until incorporated.

Gradually whisk in chicken stock and wine, then increase the heat to medium and bring to the boil, whisking occasionally. Simmer for about 2 minutes until thickened. Stir in the sour cream. Add mushrooms and beef and heat for about 1 minute to warm through. Adjust seasoning with salt and pepper and serve with noodles. Sprinkle with parsley.

Beef stroganoff is named after the great Russian gourmet, Count Grigory Stroganove (1770–1857). His chef created this dish for him when he was old and had lost all his teeth – it was the only beef dish he could chew.

LAMB CUTLETS WITH PESTO

Prep 30 minutes plus 2 hours marinating
Serves 4

¼ cup fresh lemon juice
½ teaspoon ground chilli
½ teaspoon cracked black pepper
½ teaspoon salt
1 teaspoon sumac (Middle Eastern spice
   with citrus taste)
2 cloves garlic, peeled and minced
½ cup olive oil
2 French racks of lamb, cut into cutlets
4 heaped cups fresh basil, leaves only
2 tablespoons pinenuts
2 cloves garlic
½ cup olive oil
3 heaped tablespoons Parmesan cheese, grated
salt and freshly ground black pepper to taste

Combine the lemon juice, chilli, cracked pepper, salt, sumac and garlic in a stainless-steel bowl and whisk until the salt is dissolved. Stir in the olive oil.

Lay the cutlets out on a large plate and douse the lamb cutlets in marinade on both sides. Cover and marinate for 2 hours in the refrigerator.

Place a medium-sized saucepan filled with hot water onto a high heat and bring to the boil. Place a large strainer in a bowl of ice-cold water.

Plunge the basil leaves into the boiling water and cook for 15 seconds. Remove the leaves with a skimmer and place in the iced water. Drain well and squeeze out the excess water.

Place the basil, pinenuts and garlic in a food processor and process until chopped. Pulse the processor, adding the olive oil in a thin stream while the machine is running. Add the cheese and process until blended. Season to taste with salt and pepper. Don't over-process the pesto; keep it rustic.

Heat a grill pan or barbecue to a medium-high temperature and grill the cutlets for 2 minutes each side.

Rest for 5 minutes.

Serve with a good dollop of pesto on each cutlet.

A good butcher will prepare a French rack by removing the outer layer of fat, flap and silverskin, and then cleaning the rib bones. Lamb has a delicate flavour and should always be cooked as simply as possible, with lots of garlic.

SAUSAGE STICKS WITH CARAMELISED ONION

Prep 30 minutes
Serves 4

8 short wooden skewers
1 tablespoon oil
2 large white onions, peeled and sliced into rounds
1 tablespoon brown sugar
½ teaspoon salt
¼ cup water
8 large sausages, cut into thirds
8 apricots, stoned and cut in half
juice of 2 limes
1 tablespoon ground cumin
salt and freshly ground black pepper to taste

Soak the wooden skewers in water for 2 hours.

Heat a saucepan over a medium temperature, add the oil, onions, sugar, salt and water. Cook for 20 minutes until caramelised, stirring occasionally. Set aside.

Heat the barbecue to a medium temperature.

Thread the sausage pieces and apricots alternately onto the skewers. Grill the skewers for 6–8 minutes, sprinkling lime juice and cumin on them as they cook. Season with salt and pepper.

Serve with the caramelised onion and steamed rice.

If you have a habit of burning your snarlers, or having the little guys explode into strange alien shapes, try pre-cooking them by simmering in beer for a few minutes before grilling.

lamb cutlets with pesto

CHICKEN SALAD WITH BHUJA MIX

Prep 30 minutes plus 2 hours marinating
Serves 4

¼ cup lemon juice
¼ cup gin
1 tablespoon fresh ginger, peeled and minced
1 garlic clove, minced
2 tablespoons honey
2 tablespoons oil
salt and freshly ground black pepper to taste
8 chicken thighs, skinned and boned
1 cup bhuja mix
2 ripe avocados, peeled and cut into quarters
2 tablespoons good quality maple syrup

In a bowl mix the lemon juice, gin, ginger, garlic, honey, oil and salt and pepper thoroughly. Lay the chicken out in a shallow dish and pour over the gin marinade. Cover and marinate in the refrigerator for 2 hours.

Place a grill pan on medium heat and cook the chicken thighs for 8 minutes, fat side down, and then 6 minutes on the other side. As the chicken grills, paint with the marinade. When cooked, there should be no redness in the meat.

Serve the chicken with the quartered avocado, a spoonful of bhuja mix and a drizzle of maple syrup.

Bhuja mix is an Indian-style snack food made from pea flour, rice flour, whole dried green peas, peanuts, vegetable oils, curry spices and salt. The flours are made into small noodle-like shapes that are fried in the vegetable oil. This combination just came to me out of the blue one day, and it works really well.

ROYAL CHICKEN WINGS

Prep 30 minutes
Serves 4

8 chicken wings, tips removed
½ cup thick yoghurt
2 teaspoons ginger paste
2 teaspoons garlic powder
1 teaspoon ground turmeric
juice of 1 lemon
1 teaspoon black pepper
¼ teaspoon baking soda
salt to taste
2 teaspoons sugar
2 tablespoons water
2 tablespoons flour
salt to taste
2 egg whites
4 cups peanut oil for deep frying

In a bowl mix the chicken wings with the yoghurt, ginger paste, garlic powder, turmeric, lemon juice, pepper, baking soda and salt.

Heat a large pan over medium heat and spoon the chicken wings, covered in the yoghurt mixture, into the pan. Cook on medium heat for about 6 minutes until all the liquid is absorbed, turning the wings over with tongs. Remove from heat.

In a small pan over low heat add the sugar along with two tablespoons water. Stir until the sugar is dissolved. Remove from heat, cool and add the flour, salt and egg whites and whisk until the mixture turns fluffy.

Heat the oil in a saucepan, bringing the temperature up to 180°C, and testing with a candy thermometer.

Dip each wing in the egg white batter and drop in the oil. Fry until they turn golden brown (about 10 minutes) then remove with a slotted spoon onto absorbent paper. Repeat for the remaining wings. Eight wings will need to be cooked in 2 batches. Deep-frying is not a bad cooking method as long as you don't crowd the pan. If you cook too many at once the wings will absorb the oil instead of cooking in it.

Serve with boiled potatoes, diced and sprinkled with sweet paprika.

I think chicken wings have a bad reputation as a poor man's food. This chicken dish is the favourite snack food of one of the wealthiest men in the world, so if it's good enough for a Sultan ...

GRILLED CHICKEN SANDWICHES

Prep 30 minutes
Makes 4 servings

2 tablespoons ground cumin
2 tablespoons sweet paprika
salt and freshly ground black pepper to taste
4 small chicken breasts
1 tablespoon olive oil
8 slices plain white bread
1 red onion, peeled and cut into rings
salt to taste
½ teaspoon freshly ground black pepper
juice of 2 limes
1 birdseye chilli pepper, finely sliced
½ cup coriander leaves
1 cup watercress leaves
1 tablespoon olive oil
4 squirts Kewpie Japanese mayonnaise

Heat a barbecue or grill pan on a stovetop to a medium heat.

In a small bowl mix the cumin, paprika and salt and pepper. Dip the chicken breasts in the spice rub until coated evenly, then paint them with oil.

Place the breasts on the grill and cook for 5 minutes on the first side, then turn and cook for 3 minutes on the other side. Remove from pan and place on a plate to rest for a few minutes before slicing.

Toast the bread on the grill for 1 minute each side and set aside.

In a bowl gently toss the red onion, salt, pepper, lime juice, sliced chilli, coriander leaves, watercress and oil. ▶

royal chicken wings

grilled chicken sandwiches

To serve, lay the toasted bread on plates, stack with onion salad mix, and place sliced chicken breast on the top.

Squirt a good dollop of mayonnaise around the sandwich. If you do cook the contents of this sandwich on the barbecue, and have room, cook the red onion before adding to the salad mix.

I could lie to you and say that I always make my own mayonnaise, but more often than not I use Kewpie. Look out for it in Asian supermarkets – it's the one in the super squeezy, clear plastic bottle with a baby on the front, and has a star-shaped nozzle built in.

Please be careful with me.

Sundrop
$5.95 kg

seven sweet treats

broken pavlova with lime sauce

BROKEN PAVLOVA WITH LIME SAUCE

Prep 2 hours, 30 minutes
Serves 6–8

3 egg whites
¼ teaspoon cream of tartar
1¼ cups sugar
1 teaspoon vanilla
1 teaspoon vinegar
3 teaspoons cornflour
½ cup dark rum
¼ cup molasses
4 tablespoons unsalted butter
juice of 2 limes
pinch nutmeg
4 plums, stoned and sliced

Preheat the oven to 140°C. In a clean bowl beat the egg whites with the cream of tartar until stiff. Add the sugar a little at a time, beating well after each addition. The mixture should look thick and glossy.

Now beat in the vanilla, vinegar and cornflour. Pile in a circular shape with a smooth, flat top onto greased foil on an oven tray.

Bake the pavlova in the oven for 1 hour, then turn the heat off and leave for another hour until it is cooled.

To make the lime sauce, simmer the rum and molasses in a small saucepan over a medium heat for 2 minutes. Remove from the heat and whisk in the butter, lime juice and nutmeg.

To serve, pour some of the warm lime sauce into glasses. Break up the pavlova and drop chunks on top, together with a sprinkling of plum slices.

You will find it quite satisfying just tearing the pavlova into bits. My grandmother was almost religious about how precisely she would cut hers up, using a special silver pavlova knife and measuring each portion with near surgical precision.

BLUEBERRY CRUMBLE

Prep 40 minutes
Serves 6

1 tablespoon butter for greasing
2 cups fresh breadcrumbs or brioche crumbs
2 tablespoons white sugar
1 teaspoon ground cardamom
1 teaspoon ground cinnamon
6 tablespoons unsalted butter, melted
½ cup brown sugar
2 teaspoons orange zest, finely chopped
4 cups blueberries, washed
juice of 2 oranges

Preheat the oven to 180°C. Butter the bottom of a medium-sized baking dish.

Combine the breadcrumbs, white sugar, cardamom and cinnamon in a bowl and stir in the melted butter until the breadcrumbs are evenly coated. Set aside.

In a small bowl mix the brown sugar and orange zest. Set aside.

Sprinkle ¾ cup of the breadcrumb mixture over the bottom of the baking dish. Spread ½ of the blueberries over the top.

Sprinkle ½ of the brown sugar mixture over the blueberries, then add the remaining berries and top with the rest of the brown sugar mixture.

Spread the remaining breadcrumb mixture over the top, then drizzle the orange juice over the breadcrumbs.

Bake in the preheated oven for about 30 minutes or until the breadcrumb topping is lightly browned and crisp and the blueberries begin to bubble gently. Serve warm with vanilla ice-cream.

Blueberries have been hailed as a super fruit. These sweet little berries come top of the list in neutralising the free radicals that cause ageing.

strawberry ice-cream with mango

STRAWBERRY ICE-CREAM WITH MANGO

20 minutes plus 4–6 hours freezing
Makes 8 cups

4 cups strawberries
1¼ cups white sugar
2 cups cold cream
1 cup cream
¼ cup white sugar
1 fresh mango, peeled, stoned and diced

Hull the strawberries and crush them in a bowl with 1¼ cups sugar.

Let the strawberry mash stand until the sugar is dissolved, then rub through a sieve to remove the seeds. Chill this strawberry juice in the freezer for 10 minutes.

In a container that is freezer-proof mix the strawberry juice with the 2 cups of cold cream, then freeze.

Once the strawberry cream mixture is frozen to a soft mush, whip the remaining cup of cream to soft peaks with a ¼ cup sugar.

Fold into the strawberry cream and freeze.

Scoop and serve with fresh mango.

Home-made ice-cream is something special. Kids love learning how to make it, and I like the fact that this recipe doesn't call for a $400 ice-cream machine. You could add 2 cups of diced Christmas pudding during the final stage for an unusual taste sensation.

▲ rhubarb and strawberry muffins
plum puff tart ▶

RHUBARB AND STRAWBERRY MUFFINS

Prep 40 minutes
Makes 12

oil spray
1 cup sugar
⅓ cup vegetable oil
⅔ cup buttermilk
1 large egg
2 large egg whites
1 teaspoon vanilla
1 cup diced strawberries, hulled
¾ cup rhubarb, diced
1½ cups flour
1 cup flour
1 teaspoon cinnamon
2 teaspoons baking powder
½ teaspoon baking soda
½ teaspoon salt
2 tablespoons butter, melted

Preheat the oven to 200°C. Spray a muffin tray with oil.

In a large bowl whisk the sugar, oil, buttermilk, egg, egg whites and vanilla until smooth, then set aside.

Place the strawberries and rhubarb in another bowl with ½ cup flour. Toss until well coated.

Into the buttermilk mixture add the remaining flour, cinnamon, baking powder, baking soda and salt. Use a wooden spoon to combine, then add all the flour-covered fruit. Mix well.

Spoon about ¼ cup of batter into each muffin cup. Drizzle ½ teaspoon of butter over each muffin.

Place in the centre of the oven and bake for 25 minutes or until a toothpick inserted into the centre comes out clean. Cool on a rack for 20 minutes before removing from the muffin tin.

I like tart, sharp tastes and rhubarb is one of my favourite foods. Alternatives to rhubarb are oranges, bananas, paw paw or any tropical sweet flavours.

PLUM PUFF TART

Prep 40 minutes
Makes 12

2 sheets pre-rolled puff pastry (22 x 22cm)
⅓ cup sliced almonds, toasted
4 black plums, pitted and sliced
4 apricots, pitted and sliced
3 tablespoons sugar
½ teaspoon cinnamon
juice of 1 lemon

Preheat oven to 200°C.

Thaw frozen pastry (about 10 minutes) and cut each sheet into 6 rectangles. Lay out on a baking tray.

Scatter almond slivers onto the pastry rectangles, then press the plum and apricot slices onto each rectangle, leaving a small border around the edge.

Mix the sugar and cinnamon in a small bowl. Sprinkle over the fruit tarts, then squeeze a little lemon juice over the top of each.

Bake for 25–30 minutes until the pastry is golden brown.

Serve at room temperature with whipped cream.

As a kid, plums were the number one fruit over summer and every neighbour had a plum tree to raid. They also made a great weapon as an early form of the paint ball projectile. Red plums make a hell of a mess when they splatter and for contrast white shirts were the top target.

FUDGE SAUCE AND BERRIES

Prep 20 minutes
Serves 4

¼ cup water
1 cup corn syrup
1 cup white sugar
½ teaspoon salt
½ cup unsweetened chocolate, chopped
½ cup cocoa powder (Dutch is best)
4 tablespoons unsalted butter, softened
½ cup cream
1 tablespoon vanilla essence
1 punnet strawberries
1 punnet raspberries
1 punnet blackberries

Combine the water, corn syrup and sugar in a pan on a medium heat. Bring to the boil, stirring often, until all sugar crystals have melted. Boil for a minute without stirring.

Remove from the heat and add the salt and the chocolate. Allow to stand 2 minutes until the chocolate has melted before whisking smooth.

Sift the cocoa into a mixing bowl and stir in the chocolate syrup until smooth and lump free.

Whisk in the butter, cream and vanilla until silky.

Rinse all the berries very gently and pat dry carefully with paper towels. Cut the strawberries in half.

To serve, pour a portion of the fudge sauce into small shallow bowls and spoon on the strawberries, raspberries and blackberries.

This dish is the delicious proof that simple tastes are always the best. Home-made fudge sauce will keep for a couple of months in a jar in the refrigerator. Heat in the microwave to pour over ice-cream or cake.

WALNUT FUDGE
Prep 30 minutes
Makes 20

½ cup unsweetened chocolate
1 cup brown sugar
1 cup white sugar
2 tablespoons corn syrup
⅔ cup cream
pinch salt
2 tablespoons butter
½ cup walnut pieces
1 teaspoon vanilla
1 tablespoon rum

In a saucepan over a low heat bring the chocolate, brown sugar, white sugar, corn syrup, cream and salt to the boil without stirring. Cook until a candy thermometer reaches 116°C or soft-ball stage.

Remove from the heat and cool to lukewarm, still without stirring. When cool, beat in the butter, walnuts, vanilla and rum.

Beat hard for a good 3 minutes until the fudge thickens. Spread into a pan and cut into squares before it hardens.

Make this fudge on a day when it is cool and dry and then store in an airtight container.

This fudge makes an ideal sweet to take on a romantic picnic or wrapped up as a gift at Christmas time. Make sure you buy fresh walnuts, as stale ones have a nasty rancid taste.

BUTTERSCOTCH TRIFLE
Prep 40 minutes plus 2 hours chilling
Makes 6–8 individual servings

2 cups whole milk
4 large egg yolks
½ cup sugar
¼ cup flour
2 teaspoons vanilla essence
½ cup cream
5 tablespoons unsalted butter
1 cup brown sugar
¼ cup corn syrup
4 ripe bananas, peeled and sliced
juice of 1 lemon
1 small sponge cake (20cm), cut into 4cm dice
home-made jellies to garnish

To make the custard, heat the milk in a saucepan over a medium heat until hot but not boiling. Remove from the heat and set aside.

In a medium-sized bowl combine the egg yolks, sugar and flour and whisk until smooth. Slowly add the warm milk to the egg mixture, whisking as you pour. Pour the mixture into the saucepan and cook for about 3 minutes over a low heat, stirring until the mixture boils and thickens.

Strain the mixture into a bowl and stir in the vanilla. Allow the custard to cool to room temperature.

For the butterscotch sauce, heat the cream, butter, brown sugar and corn syrup in a saucepan over a low heat, stirring until the butter melts.

Stirring constantly, increase the heat to bring the mixture to a boil. Remove the pan from the heat and set aside to cool to room temperature.

Before you begin to assemble the trifle, combine the banana slices with the lemon juice and set aside.

Line the bottom of 6 small bowls with the diced cake, overlapping each slice slightly. Spread the banana slices over the cake layer. Pour the butterscotch sauce over the bananas. Spoon the custard over the butterscotch sauce.

Depending on the size of your bowls, you may not use up all the butterscotch sauce or custard on the layers. Try for even amounts of each.

Cover and refrigerate for at least 2 hours or preferably overnight.

Serve the individual trifles garnished with jelly or whipped cream.

butterscotch trifle

VANILLA CUPCAKES

Prep 40 minutes
Makes 12

½ cup butter, softened
1 cup white sugar
3 large eggs, separated
1 teaspoon vanilla essence
1 cup white flour
1 teaspoon baking powder
½ teaspoon baking soda
¼ teaspoon salt
½ cup buttermilk
1½ cups icing sugar
1 teaspoon butter, softened
2 teaspoons lemon juice
1½ tablespoons hot water

Preheat the oven to 180°C. Line a medium-sized muffin tin with 12 paper baking cups.

In a large bowl use an electric hand-mixer to beat the butter with the sugar until white and fluffy. Now beat in the egg yolks and vanilla. Set aside.

Into another bowl sift the flour, baking powder, baking soda and salt. Set aside.

In a large stainless-steel bowl whisk the egg whites until soft peaks form.

Using a wooden spoon stir the flour mixture and buttermilk alternately into the butter mixture. Gently fold in the egg whites.

Spoon the batter into the baking cups.

Bake in the middle of the oven for 30 minutes or until a testing skewer comes out clean. Cool on a wire rack before icing.

For the icing, sift the icing sugar into a bowl, add the butter and lemon juice and beat with a wooden spoon. Add the hot water a little at a time until the mixture becomes smooth and spreadable. Ice the cupcakes and garnish with sprinkles.

Cupcakes were one of the first bakery items I cooked at manual school, only mine had butterfly wings and jelly on top. I learned the power of food very early on – I traded my cupcakes for kisses from Rachel Clark.

CHOCOLATE BALLS

Prep 20 minutes
Makes 12 balls

4 tablespoons good quality cocoa
2 cups icing sugar
½ cup whisky
¼ cup corn syrup
2½ cups crushed plain vanilla wine biscuits
1 cup nuts, chopped (pecans, macadamias or hazelnuts)
½ cup icing sugar, extra

In a large bowl sift the cocoa and icing sugar together. Add the whisky and corn syrup and mix until combined.

Fold in the crushed vanilla wine biscuits and nuts and mix thoroughly.

With your hands, shape the chocolate dough into small balls, then roll in icing sugar. Store in an airtight container.

Variations on this recipe include adding crystallised ginger, hokey pokey, marshmallow, coconut, peanut butter, gingernuts or cherries.

chocolate balls

the author at work ...

WEIGHT CONVERSIONS

25gms	1oz
50gms	2oz
100gms	3½oz
200gms	7oz
300gms	10½oz
400gms	14oz
450gms	16oz (1lb)
500gms	17½oz
750gms	26½oz
1kg	35oz

LIQUID CONVERSIONS

5ml	1 tspn
15ml	1 tblspn
30ml	⅛ cup
60ml	¼ cup
125ml	½ cup
150ml	⅔ cup
175ml	¾ cup
250ml	1 cup
500ml	2 cups
600ml	1 pint

LENGTH CONVERSIONS

1cm	½ inch
2.5cm	1 inch
5cm	2 inches
10cm	4 inches
20cm	8 inches
30cm	12 inches / 1 foot

TEMPERATURE CONVERSIONS

Celsius	Fahrenheit	Gas
100	225	¼
125	250	½
150	300	2
160	325	3
170	325	3
180	350	4
190	375	5
200	400	6
210	425	7
220	425	7
230	450	8
250	500	9

ROASTING TIME FOR MEAT, COOKED AT 200°C INTERNAL MEAT TEMPERATURE MEASURED WITH A MEAT THERMOMETER

Beef

Rare	60°C
Medium	70°C
Well done	80°C

Pork

Medium	80°C
Well done	85°C

Lamb

Medium	70°C
Well done	80°C

The exact measurements in the tables have been rounded for convenience.

PENGUIN BOOKS

Penguin Books (NZ) Ltd, cnr Airborne and Rosedale Roads,
Albany, Auckland 1310, New Zealand
Penguin Books Ltd, 80 Strand, London, WC2R 0RL, England
Penguin Putnam Inc, 375 Hudson Street, New York, NY 10014,
United States
Penguin Books Australia Ltd, 250 Camberwell Road, Camberwell,
Victoria 3124, Australia
Penguin Books Canada Ltd, 10 Alcorn Avenue, Toronto,
Ontario, Canada M4V 3B2
Penguin Books (South Africa) (Pty) Ltd, 24 Sturdee Avenue,
Rosebank, Johannesburg 2196, South Africa
Penguin Books India (P) Ltd, 11, Community Centre, Panchsheel Park,
New Delhi 110 017, India
Penguin Books Ltd, Registered Offices: Harmondsworth, Middlesex, England

First published by Penguin Books (NZ) Ltd, 2002

1 3 5 7 9 10 8 6 4 2

Copyright text and photographs © Garth Hokianga, 2002

The right of Garth Hokianga to be identified as the author of this work in
terms of section 96 of the Copyright Act 1994 is hereby asserted.

Designed and typeset by Athena Sommerfeld
Printed by Bookbuilders, Hong Kong

The publisher wishes to thank Freedom Furniture for the use of the table and
chairs in the photograph on the front cover.

ISBN 0 14 301836 1
www.penguin.co.nz